Common Sense

(modernized)

© 2012 Jonathan Girgis, Huntington Beach, CA

Printed in the United States of America.

Written by a person who is concerned.

Written by a person who is part of the future generation.

Special Thanks to:

Marina High School's one and only Professor Earl J. Ziemann. I can't thank you enough. There are a lot of things in this book that you talked about in U.S. History and World Geography class.

Professor Jean Legere of Economics and Government, who also works at Marina High School. You make economics so interesting!

Mom and Dad and Justin and Josh.

Ms. Virginia Clifford, a true inspiration.

J.B., for not running me over on that one Friday in September.

Table of Contents

Introduction

January 1775: America

Trouble is stirring. The colonists living in the original thirteen colonies are angry. And for good reason: for some time, King George III and his Parliament have been quite paternalistic towards their New World possession. After the French and Indian War, the British Empire is facing a financial dilemma. Debt has piled up during the seven years of war against the hated French. The British, refusing to tax their own nobility, decide to lay the task upon their "children," the Americans. But these kids don't like to be treated this way. Taxes on their tea, paper, and even the prohibition of paper money are seen as being unacceptable.

Dependence must end ASAP, these people think. The fighting soon begins.

***

A year after war commenced, a man named Thomas Paine arrived on the scene with a pamphlet he wrote named, "*Common Sense*." It became a national bestseller. In *Common Sense*, Paine provided multiple reasons for why the colonists needed to unite against the oppressive power of the monarch. He wanted a system of government where the rights and representation of citizens were implemented. He also wished to inform the public about the main issues the American people faced at that time. Similarly, after only, well, about 236 years, this book seeks to do the same. Just like *Common Sense*, this book has been written using simple language. In *Common Sense*, Thomas Paine showed a brilliant ability to notify and enlighten readers about the America they live in, and this book aims to be just as interesting, revealing, and relevant, and it will be focusing on the war we've been in for the past decade. It details my viewpoint on a number of issues and problems that the United States faces. I urge you to go beyond the covers of this book and search for more information yourself on this topic that concerns you. In other words, be informed. Be involved. Do not be ignorant or easily deceived by what you see on TV or in the news. You're better than that. Use the internet and other resources to help you out. This book can only do so much. I don't want to keep you reading this intro for too long, so I'll

stop here. Without further ado, best of luck and get ready
for something essential.

Yours truly,

Jonathan Girgis

"I, however, place economy among the first and most important republican virtues, and public debt as the greatest of the dangers to be feared."
-Thomas Jefferson

Economics 101

If Jefferson believed that economics is important, we should think so too. But first, what *is* economics? According to Dictionary.com, economics is the "the science that deals with the production, distribution, and consumption of goods and services (in a market economy), or the material welfare of humankind." There are two major economic policies that I will discuss here. These are:

- Keynesian economics

and

- Supply side economics

Unless you're studying economics right now or you're majoring in business, you probably don't know what these two things are; they may as well be written in

Chinese. However, neither term is too hard to comprehend. In Keynesian economics, you spend money, not save it. John Keynes, who developed this theory primarily during the Great Depression, stated that there should be a good level of money circulating in the economy. Overall, it's all about both personal and national (in terms of government) spending. More spending supposedly increases economic growth. But here's the problem: the Keynesian economic theory is really short- term thinking.

> *Overall, economics is all about personal and national (in terms of government) spending.*

It was meant for stimulating the American economy during the Great Depression (World War II really did the job, though) but it wasn't meant for long-term policy. And a fundamental detail of Keynesian economics is spending, but where does the money come from? It can come from taxes or printing money, but both of these things are looked at negatively by common people. Supply side economics is also known as "Reagonomics" or "trickle-down" economics. There are certain parts to supply side economics,including deregulation and tax cuts. Developed by former president Ronald Reagan (term in office: 1981-1989), supply side economics focuses on giving money to the wealthy in America so that they can pass, or trickle down, wealth to the lower classes in society. In other words, this economic theory bluntly coins the wealthy as the "job creators." The Republican Party still uses that term today. I haven't really seen Donald Trump (billionaire) creating jobs for the middle class at the moment, did you? When you hear "Bill Gates," you think about Microsoft, billionaire, rich guy, and maybe even his nonprofit organization, but do you think of a man who has taken action to make jobs for the other 99%? In general, the wealthy in this country have *not* created jobs for others. Trickle -down economics doesn't really work. If rich folks are given money, they use it for themselves.

Nowadays, the gap between the rich and the poor has grown noticeably. Moreover, class conflicts are on the rise. Back in 1786, a farmer named Daniel Shay organized other fellow farmers during a time of economic downturn and tough government policies. This rebellion really scared the rich.

They saw what looked like a simple group of rural farmers instead as being a potential threat to their interests. Today, the same perspective of the affluent applies. This 1% of the nation's people want to keep the other 99% in check. Seriously. It's been that way since the beginning of American history: keep the "rubble," meaning the middle and low classes, apart, not unified. The Pew Research Center made a recent study in 2011 of how Americans perceived class conflicts. Surprisingly, out 2,048 adults, 66% of them believed that class conflicts were either strong or very strong.

There is also macro- and microeconomics. Macro economics is "big" economics, focusing on the consumer spending and production of the economy in general. Microeconomics, or "small" economics, focuses on things like individual decision making. Anyways, a couple of different things need to be identified. One is boom and bust cycles. Here there is a rise in economic growth, and then there's a fall in economic growth. The greater the rise in the economy, the greater the bust. Simple. In addition, supply and demand are part of boom and bust cycles. If there's a low demand for a product, whether there's enough of it or not, the price of the product will be low. If there's a high demand for a certain product while the supply of it is low, the *price* of the product will be high. Supply and demand influence industry in dramatic ways. More demand for a product causes the industry producting it to work to meet that demand. So if everyone starts buying Ford cars, then the Ford Company would have to increase its production (to meet the demand). It can do so by hiring more workers, for example. Then let's say that soon people find out that Ford cars are continuously having major engine problems, and so consumers would refuse to buy the car.

An important event occurred in 2009, when General Motors (GM) had to be bailed out by the U.S. government, which payed $50 billion to save the American multinational company. The President, Barack Obama, who presented the plan to rescue GM, in my opinion, was striking in making that decision. Think about it. How many things go into building a car? Without GM, lots of people would be out of work.

This would be detrimental to the company, which is now going to lose profit because less people are buying Ford cars. The company would have to take measures to try to sell as many cars as possible (through more advertising, discounts, etc.). If profit still continues to decrease, then it would probably start laying off workers, causing the number of people unemployed to rise, and this would happen until bankruptcy is declared. This is what is happening to American Apparel, a clothing manufacturer in the U.S. Low demand for its products and increasing decline in sales has caused the company to attempt reversing its problems by much advertising using models and such. If things don't change positively, American Apparel could go out of business, putting many people out of work as well.

Michael Moore, a brilliant film maker, made a documentary in 2003 about corporations. Did you know that in the U.S., corporations are legally people?

Lastly, free trade is a concept you need to be familiar with. Free trade is the idea that the government does not interfere with imports coming in from foreign countries or exports with exports leaving the country. If you've noticed how so many American companies like American Apparel are struggling to survive or how so many others have gone out of business or moved overseas, the problem is kind of because of free trade. American labor cannot compete with foreign labor that pays 10 cents an hour. It's impossible. End of story. And corporations want maximum profit, even if it means exploiting the resources of foreign countries and using child labor. Lower salaries, more profit. Nothing else matters to corporate interests than profit. Period. Some people might point out that free trade leads to cheaper prices due to the cheaper labor being used. But this is controversial because with more jobs being lost (outsourcing) you have higher unemployment, which leads to less people buying a product. So is free trade necessarily a good thing? For countries like China, the "Rising Dragon," the answer would be yes. Massive numbers of corporations have moved to China because of its cheap and very large labor source (huge potential in a country with a population of over 1 billion people) and lenient regulation. As a result, the country has industrialized rapidly and its middle class has been growing. Right now China has the second largest economy in the world. Could have the best one in the future. So is free trade bad for everybody? The answer to *that* question would be no.

Common Sense: Both Keynesian and supply side economics have their problems. Boom and bust cycles (non-ending) and supply/demand go hand-in-hand.

Since the 1800's.

"America will never be destroyed from the outside. If we falter and lose our freedoms, it will be because we destroyed ourselves."

-Abraham Lincoln

The American Government

Benjamin Franklin, after he helped form the newly formed Constitution, was asked by a woman named Mrs. Powel if the new American government was of a republic or a monarchy. His reply, "A republic, madam, if you can keep it." That's still a statement that should echo in our minds today. But can we keep our republic? Or will it fall apart?

See, America is an experiment. It's been that way for the past 200 years. Additionally, America is unique. It showed the world back in the 18th century that you didn't need a monarch to rule people with an iron fist. People could rule themselves. You could have a government where people were significant as well. Consequently, the first three words in the preamble of the Constitution, "We The People," show how important citizens are in this country. In other words, our government *is* the people, *for* the people, *by* the people. But there's a problem: sadly, that isn't really the case today.

***

The United States has a federal government that is divided into three branches: executive, judicial, and legislative.

Executive power is held by the president. Judicial power is held by the federal courts and led by the Supreme Court. Legislative power is held by Congress, which consists of the House of Representatives and the Senate. Put in place by the Constitution, checks and balances make sure that no single branch of government gains too much power. I want to specifically focus on the legislative branch of government. In our Congress today, there seems to be a battle going on, a conflict between two key parties: Republican and Democratic.

What does the Republican Party believe in? The Republican Party, also known as the "Grand Old Party," whose symbol is the elephant, is conservative (cautious towards change; right side of the political spectrum), it supports limited government, big business, tax cuts (supposedly, more taxes will discourage people from working), and increased spending on the military. The Grand Old Party tends to go against gay marriage and abortion. This is for a majority of Republicans. The

Republican Party is dominant in the South and Midwestern states. Examples of Republicans who have had or still have political power include Abraham Lincoln, Ronald Reagan, George W. Bush, and Mitt Romney. And then there's the Democratic Party.

What does the Democratic Party believe in? The Democratic Party, whose symbol is the donkey, tends to be more liberal (tolerant of change/different views; left side of the political spectrum), it usually supports decreased spending on the military, legalization of abortion and same-sex marriage, and a decrease in military spending. The Democratic Party is dominant in the Northeast of the United States. Examples of Democrats who have had or still have political power are Andrew Jackson, Franklin Delano Roosevelt, Jimmy Carter, and Barack Hussein Obama. As stated earlier, there is a clash of Republicans and Democrats. Imagine a tug-of-war between a group of Democrats and a group of Republicans for the purpose of achieving dominance in the federal government. This fight is for an attempt to gain control in Congress and the presidency.

> In election time, lots of people blame the president for economic problems in the U.S. as if it was all his fault. but don't forget: there's a Congress (and a Supreme Court) that has power as well.

The side wins because it has more influence, more money, more rhetoric, and when it comes to presidential campaigns, usually more negative campaigning (from money donations), which establishes the weakness and mistakes of an opponent, who is usually the candidate of the opposite party. You see negative campaigning, which spikes around October and November during the election period, in advertisements by means of television, billboards, and other signs and communication (for instance, RepubliCAN vs. DemocRAT). Negative campaigning typically consists of the picture of the victim and a phrase that the political incumbent, and then a comment by a narrator on how that person, for instance, the current president, is wrong.

Common Sense: America is special. Let's keep it that way. Our political leaders need to realize what's good for the country, for the 99%, not just to fight for seats in the political system. It's about time to cooperate. Big corporations like Monsanto, which specialize in making genetically modified seeds, aren't the ones who should be represented in Congress. No more corporate lobbyism! More citizen representation!

This conflict mentioned earlier between Democrats and Republicans has been around for a long time. Today, it's damaging. Congress itself is having its own "Civil War," and little compromise is being reached. This partisan gridlock in our law-making branch of government is horrible. Congress declines to work together with the president. Good thing? No, no, no. Republican or Democrat, liberal or conservative, enough is enough. These Congressmen and Congresswomen need to do what's good for the country, basing their decisions on the positions and interests of the citizens of the United States. I do not think that too many people support our fighting in the Middle East, yet Congress and the president are responsible for signing the military budget annually. No signatures, no war anymore. If our Congressmen and Congresswomen really did represent our interests, I don't think they would commit billions of dollars to defense and military. The U.S. has the largest military budget in the world. Just think about what we could do with that type of money. The possibilities are nearly endless. I criticize this lack of progress and this lack of the peoples' representation. The citizens and the government should be inseparable; they are one. Corporations and other self interests shouldn't be part of this model. The government is not to be some separate entity that disregards its own people. The power of the government lies within the people. Our government is not totalitarian, and our leader is not a monarch. We have rights, and opinions, and they must be considered and represented. If special interests are replacing us in the minds of our representatives, then it's time for a change in their thinking.

In other words, you must be willing to stand up for what you believe in. Being complacent and ignoring the current situation is your choice, but it won't benefit you or anyone else. Perhaps you're familiar with Martin Luther King Jr., Harriet Beecher Stowe, and Harriet Tubman. Despite the hard circumstances they were in, these remarkable people refused to be stopped from pushing for change. These are the type of people that

Common Sense: Do your duty as an American. Participate in politics, vote, and stand up for your beliefs. Don't let corporations and other interests take what belongs to you: representation. We need to stop blaming others for our problems. We, together, can incite change.

history still remembers and applauds. And these are the type of people we need today.

> Common Sense: Do your duty as an American. Participate in politics, vote, and stand up for your beliefs. Don't let corporations and other interests take what belongs to you: representation. We need to stop blaming others for our problems. We, together, can incite change.

"All wars are civil wars, because all men are brothers."
-Francois Fenelon

"Every gun that is made, every warship launched, every rocket fired, signifies in the final sense a theft from those who hunger and are not fed, those who are cold and are not clothed."

-Dwight D. Eisenhower

"It has too often been too easy for rulers and governments to incite man to war."

- Lester B. Pearson

The Long War

This is big. Here Francois, a poet and theologian who experienced one of the greatest European wars, the

War of the Spanish Succession, reveals his inner feelings concerning war. Dwight D. Eisenhower, five-star general in World War II and former U.S. president, profoundly maintains how war is wasteful and damaging. Lester Pearson, former Canadian professor and prime minister, says something that everyone needs to know and commit to memory. This chapter will focus on the Long War, the "War on Terror."

September 11, 2001. You all know the story. Terrorists came to the United States, trained here, and then hijacked planes and flew two of them into the Twin Towers in New York, leading to the buildings' destruction, and flew another into part of the Pentagon, and one into a field in Pennsylvania after the passengers rose up and fought against the hijackers. May sound simple, but there's more. American people asked after the attack, "Why? Why do they hate us?"

Former President George W. Bush used the catastrophic event to his advantage (recall what Pearson said-see p. 25). So Bush sent this country off to war and the military to hell, where after 11 years, it's still there. But let's briefly center our attention to the Middle East. You hear about this place all the time now. This region in the world consists of Arabs, meaning people who are of Arab origin or speak the Arab language. Most of the inhabitants who live there are Muslims, followers of Islam, a religion that was founded by the prophet Mohammed. The majority of Muslims are Sunni Muslims. The minority, the Shi'ite, don't like Sunni Muslims too much. While Saddam Hussein, a Sunni Muslim himself and former Iraqi dictator, was in power, he oppressed the Shi'ite Muslims (80% of the population at that time) living in Iraq. Point proven.

Read *The Kite Runner* by Khaled Hosseini. You will understand an accurate Afghani viewpoint of the conditions in Afghanistan.

More significantly, however, is the topic of terrorism. Some people think that all Muslims are terrorists. That isn't true. Only a small percentage of Muslims are terrorists. Nowadays, it seems like all terrorists are Muslims. These terrorists believe that they are struggling against the West and its ideals in a crusade they call, "Jihad." Westerners see terrorists as evil, inhumane, and mentally troubled. The terrorists see themselves as Muslim martys fighting and dying for a holy cause, and in return they end up going to paradise. But myself personally I feel there's more to this than just deep religious conviction, which these people do have. I mean, there are religious Muslims that aren't terrorists, so what's the idea?

I advise you to look at things from their perspective. For instance, how much conviction do you need to have in order to strap bombs to your body to kill someone while killing yourself in the process? It takes an enormous amount of passion for a cause and belief; killing oneself or someone else isn't easy. That's what these terrorists have- a huge amount of conviction in what they believe in (Allah, paradise, and the West is the enemy). They're radically motivated to do what they do.

Ooh, yes, radicalism. What's that? According to Dictionary.com, radicalism is the, "political orientation of those who favor revolutionary change in government and society." These Muslim terrorists are radical, and so is the Taliban, Shariah law, etc. Now, there's really nothing anyone can do about it.

Well, maybe something can be done.

After World War II, the through the brilliant Marshall Plan, the United States was able to thwart radicalism in Western Europe. What was the Marshall Plan? It was an *economic* stimulus that provided funding for infrastructure and was able to rebuild the western part of Europe. Key point: Out of desperation and misery comes radicalism.

Know this: In the Middle East, there are three common things: sand, poverty, and pollution. Before becoming a terrorist, that Middle Eastern person probably wasn't living a happy life. Things weren't going right at all. The chances that a typical man from Afghanistan, Pakistan, or Iraq will receive a high school level education of some sort are slim, and for a college education, almost non-existent. And without a college degree, which would lead to a professional career, that person is stuck in an impoverished condition. So, you think that somebody living in Afghanistan, for example, who makes a couple of dollars a day is somehow living like a prince or even like a middle class person? In general, these people are very poor and desperate. Desperate people do desperate things. I firmly believe that desperation (an individualized economic problem) is a key starting point for why there is always a Middle

Eastern terrorist out there. The majority of terrorists weren't/aren't educated people with professional careers that pay well. With little to no hope in life, flying planes into buildings to find a sure way to get to a better place, once again, called paradise seems like a good idea. If you remember pre-WWII history, Germany of the early 20th century wasn't doing well economically. The Treaty of Versailles that Germany was placed under as punishment for partly causing World War I imposed large restrictions and penalties, and as a people altogether, Germans were not happy. What happened not too far ahead? Out of this sense of hopelessness and desperation came the man you all know of as Adolf Hitler. To the Germans, Hitler was a savior, a leader capable of making Germany great again, and the Germans had a strong sense of loyalty to him and followed under his direction through World War II. And

Hitler was also a "terrorist." He helped lead to the deaths of almost 11 millon people; 6 million of them were Jews, and 5 million consisted of other people. Likewise, Muslim terrorists have helped cause the deaths of Westerners and Christians. Hitler used his Nazi death camps to eliminate his enemies; Muslim terrorists use guns, bombs, and even planes to eliminate their enemies. Hitler followed a radical ideology; Muslims follow a radical ideology too. Both of these two people came from places and environments that had bad conditions. You see, people always have a tendency to try to get of a miserable condition if they can do so. Fight in a world war? Sure. Kill someone else? Why not. Kill a plane full of people? If that's what it takes. So is there a real way to get rid of radicalism? Is there a real way to lower crime rates anywhere in the world, including here in the U.S.? Yeah. Consider taking away desperation and hopelessness like that which many Middle Eastern people suffer, and-ding, ding, ding!-we've got a very possible answer. I'm sure there would be a much lower number of men applying for a job of suicide and slaughter, if they have Opportunity and Hope.

In December of 2011, the American conflict in Iraq finally ended. But so many of our troops are still in Afghanistan (90,000 over there), Saudi Arabia, and other foreign countries like Japan.

People in the U.S. stereotypically associate black people as being criminals and gangsters. Black people, in general, live a "life of crime." Well, consider this. For a black kid living in downtown Los Angeles who has to go to an awful school, knowing that his chances of success later on in life are minimal, selling drugs to people and making big bucks doesn't seem to be a bad idea. And so for terrorists, similarly, joining a "gang" of terrorists doesn't seem to be such a bad idea when life stinks, most likely won't improve, and there are rewards later on (paradise, remember).

And finally, if you've seen the movie of Captain America lately, there's a really interesting quote spoken by one of the bad guys as he is dying in the hands of Captain America, "Cut off one head, and two more shall take its place." More realistically, I think this can apply to this subject matter. On May 2, 2011, Osama Bin Laden was killed by U.S. Navy SEALS. People, especially here in America, were overjoyed to hear that the man accused of plotting September 11 was finally dead. Not to disappoint, but see, simply because one terrorist, main leader like Bin Laden or not, is killed, it's not as if all the other terrorists are going to lay aside their weapons and quit. This is not some medieval battle where the general dies and everyone else surrenders. It's the exact opposite of that. "Two more heads" will take Bin Laden's place. This battle is not over. And it will never be as long as we continue to approach this problem, this threat, with the wrong mindset.

American military casualties in

Afghanistan:

2,000

Of those:

40.2% died from explosive devices.

30.6% died from hostile fire.

In recent years, both political incumbents, President Barack Obama and Mitt Romney, were asked something like this, "Should the U.S. end the war in Afghanistan?" Both answered, "No, not until all U.S. military leaders are confident the mission has been accomplished." Um, what *mission*? Over forty terrorist attempts against the

U.S. have been foiled because of citizens and major intelligence operations, not because of this conflict. I want to stress this: You don't win a war on terrorism by sending troops, from a country like the United States that is already despised by many Middle Easterners, into Middle Eastern territory, and then have those troops fight and kill those Middle Easterners. By doing just that, the problem gets *worse*. It's like I don't like you at all. Then all of a sudden you get on my front yard without asking my permission, decide to camp there, and if I even try to do anything to push you off, you're heavily armed, so that wouldn't be a smart idea. Then you kill one of my close family members. How would I feel in the end? If it was anything, I would want to kill *you*. In fact, I could find a number of ways to do so. More realistically, those are feelings of many Afghanistan, Pakistani, and Iraqi people. Hard feelings.

So many of their mostly innocent people, family and friends, have been killed. So you can only expect retaliation. Those people in this region want American troops that we hold so dear, they want them out. And you should too. I'm not trying to put the American military in a negative aspect. I appreciate these brave men and womens' service. But for the greater good of the people, and our self interests, I advise that it's time to cut back. How about taking that money we put into war and putting it here at home, in our government programs?

Lastly, in reference to the War on Terror, many people living in the United States don't even know why American troops are in the Middle East right now (once more, what's this mission Obama and Romney are talking about?). I believe this War has lost much support since it began in 2001. Although fighting terrorism and terrorist groups has to be the main reason a majority of troops overseas are in the Middle East, here is one suggested and implied reason of why American troops are fighting overseas:

"He who is the author of a war lets loose the whole contagion of hell and opens a vein that bleeds a nation to death."

-Thomas Paine

Some people argue that soldiers are there in order to protect our oil interests. Since we do use oil (a nonrenewable resource) at an explosive rate, that seems to be the answer. But here are the facts: the top two main places of our foreign oil source are Canada and Mexico. Middle Eastern countries are lower on the list. Interestingly, the U.S. hasn't placed soldiers in Canada as much as those placed in the Middle East. Is our involvement in the Middle East becuase of oil. No. Why? Answer: **Because whoever has oil has to sell it.** You can't do anything with it if it's just sitting there, and it won't do anything for you!! If I'm a Saudi Arabian guy with an oil field, what good is it to me if I just keep that field instead of having Exxon Mobil take it to extract oil and in return pay me handsomely?

Our oil interests can't be the answer as to why the U.S. is there.

Really, American troops are fighting in the Middle East in order to try to fight (Muslim) terrorism. It may seem that if we increase the budget of the military and have more military men in the Middle East there will be less terrorist attacks. This may seem reasonable, but since September 2001, there have been over twenty attempted terrorist attacks against America.

Bottom line is this: the War on Terror is not working. Most, if not all, wars are destructive and useless. There are ways to avoid war. Peace is part of the answer to solving a conflict such as this one. You can't win terrorism with more money or more weapons or more soldiers (we've already tried that). Killing and imprisoning innocent Middle Easterners and/or Muslim terrorists isn't going to help in the long run. If you want to fight terrorism, then focus on the economic situation of the people living in the Middle Eastern region; instead, by killing their people, America is hated even more by these Muslim Middle Easterners. This "War on Terror" is wasteful in terms of money and lives. Enough is enough! We have to attend to more important domestic issues back here at home. And don't say we don't have any of *those*. Moreover, we need to grasp the fact that our troops do have value. Like any war, this war is a waste of good men on both sides. Let's put an end to any more heartache of mothers, fathers, wives, and children who could lose a loved one in this useless war.

When this war is over, America will not be the winner. Sadly, this country will be the loser who has lost so much.

Common Sense: Let's Get Out! Now!!

"A people that values its privileges above its principles soon loses both."
-Dwight D. Eisenhower

Final Note

You've probably heard this a couple of times, but it's true. At times, people living in the United States take their living conditions, their rights, and their liberties for granted. Many Americans live their everyday lives forgetting that, in comparison to the majority of other human beings living somewhere else, they are beyond doubt blessed. Lots of people complain about things that range from a minor headache to video games to their own personal jobs. I myself do that complaining at times. But it is really important to realize just how lucky you are to be where you are right now. Whenever you think things are going downhill, remember that there's always someone out there whose suffered worse. I'm not necessarily encouraging you or anyone else to be satisfied with a low state of affairs, but in my opinion, always be thankful. Thanksgiving Day should not be the only day that you are grateful for what you have: the freedom of speech, religion, press, etc.

Secondly, it's true that freedom is not free. But it's also true that your rights are not free. Hundreds of years ago American patriots laid down their lives so that the country you live in would be without suppressive rule and limited rights. There are powerful people and companies who wish to take those rights away from you, a citizen of the U.S; these are corporations and other special interests. Know your rights, and fight to preserve them. When the Constitution says that Congressmen and women must represent your interests, then they must do so. It's their responsibility. But I think it's also your responsibility to ensure that your representatives and senators represent you. If people sit around doing nothing about lobbyism and corruption in Congress, then there will be no change. As part of the government, citizens must not ignore their duties. What duties? Voting, obeying laws, and paying taxes are all things every real American citizen should do.

Lastly, on a final note, I find it hard to ignore the fact that there are quite a number of wrong things with our society in general. I'm not saying everyone's a bad person, but there seems to be a decline in people's attitudes, thinking, and behavior. I mean, I could only feel furious when I saw a video of a couple of kids on a bus teasing and insulting an elderly woman who was minding her own business. I was troubled to hear about a guy who went into a theater in Arizona and shoots a bunch of people who were there to watch a movie. I'd be amazed to find someone who hasn't seen someone else get flipped off while driving in Los Angeles. I was utterly disgusted when I heard about one guy eating another guy in Florida. Things seem to be going out of control morally in this country. This trend in immoral actions and ways needs to be reduced and discussed. As a nation and a people, we are better than this. We make mistakes, but we need to learn to get back up and continue life in the most productive and impacting way. Doing community service, going on a Peace Corp mission, and such are some of the ways that people like you and me can make a postive difference. In the end, we'll not only be proud Americans, but Americans who have left a legacy behind. A legacy that is to be remembered by others. So, friend, what difference are you making?

Definitions

Economic growth: a rise in the goods and services produced in an economy.

Boom and bust cycles: rise and fall in business cycle. Recessions, depressions, and economic growth are part of this cycle.

Terrorists: people who use violence and threats for a cause.

Marshall Plan: economic stimulus put in place to help rebuild Western Europe.

U.S. Constitution: the Supreme Law of the Land of the United States.

Congress: legislative branch of government. Consists of the House of Representatives and the Senate. Role includes making laws, declaring war, paying for defense, and collecting taxes.

Thomas Paine: author of "Common Sense." One of the founding fathers of the United States.

Checks and Balances: balance of power outlined in Constitution to prevent one single branch of government (legislative, judicial, or executive) from gaining too much power.

Radicalism: extreme perspective on an idea/belief.

Supply and Demand: Supply and demand have a direct relationship. Lower price=higher demand. Supply increases to meet demand.

Free Trade: trade without restrictions between countries.

Islam: religion founded by Mohammed. Followers of this religion are called Muslims.

Sources

"10 Facts About US Withdrawal from Afghanistan." *10 Facts About the US Withdrawal from Afghanistan*. N.p., n.d. Web. 07 Oct. 2012. http://countdowntodrawdown.org/facts.php .

"Abraham Lincoln Quotes." *BrainyQuote*. Xplore, n.d. Web. 07 Oct. 2012. http://www.brainyquote.com/quotes/authors/a/abraham_lincoln.html .

"Adams vs. Jefferson: The Birth of Negative Campaigning in the U.S. - Mental Floss." *Adams vs. Jefferson: The Birth of Negative Campaigning in the U.S. - Mental Floss*. N.p., n.d. Web. 07 Oct. 2012. http://www.mentalfloss.com/blogs/archives/141192 .

"Afghanistan War, 11 Years On: What More Can and Should the US Military Do?" *The Christian Science Monitor*. The Christian Science Monitor, 07 Oct. 2012. Web. 07 Oct. 2012. http://www.csmonitor.com/USA/Military/2012/1007/Afghanistan-war-11-years-on-What-more-can-and-should-the-US-military-do .

Avlon, John. "Forty-Five Foiled Terror Plots Since 9/11." *The Daily Beast*. Newsweek/Daily Beast, 08 Sept. 2011. Web. 07 Oct. 2012. http://www.thedailybeast.com/articles/2011/09/08/9-11-anniversary-45-terror-plots-foiled-in-last-10-years.html .

"Benjamin Franklin Quotes." *LibertyQuotes*. N.p., n.d. Web. 07 Oct. 2012. http://quotes.liberty-tree.ca/quotes_by/benjamin franklin .

"Captain America Movie Quotes:Good Mixture of Superhero Ingredients(Total Quotes: 90)." *Captain America Movie Quotes*. N.p., n.d. Web. 07 Oct. 2012. http://www.moviequotesandmore.com/captain-america-movie-quotes.html .

"China GDP Growth Rate." *China GDP Growth Rate*. N.p., n.d. Web. 07 Oct. 2012. http://www.tradingeconomics.com/china/gdp-growth .

"Comparison of Sunni and Shia Islam." *Comparison Chart of Sunni and Shia Islam*. N.p., n.d. Web. 07 Oct. 2012. http://www.religionfacts.com/islam/comparison_charts/islamic_sects.htm .

"Daniel Shays." *Shays' Rebellion*. N.p., n.d. Web. 07 Oct. 2012. http://shaysrebellion.stcc.edu/shaysapp/person.do?shortName=daniel_shays .

"DealBook." *DealBook*. N.p., n.d. Web. 07 Oct. 2012. http://dealbook.nytimes.com/2011/04/01/american-apparel-warns-of-bankruptcy/ .

"Democrat vs Republican Party." - *Difference and Comparison*. N.p., n.d. Web. 07 Oct. 2012. http://www.diffen.com/difference/Democrat_vs_Republican .

"Dwight D. Eisenhower Quotes." *BrainyQuote*. Xplore, n.d. Web. 07 Oct. 2012. http://www.brainyquote.com/quotes/authors/d/dwight_d_eisenhower.html .

"Economic Cycle (redirected from Boom-and-Bust Cycles)." *TheFreeDictionary.com*. N.p., n.d. Web. 07 Oct. 2012. http://financial-dictionary.thefreedictionary.com/Boom-and-Bust%20Cycles .

"Economics Basics: Supply and Demand." *Investopedia – Educating the World about Finance*. N.p., n.d. Web. 07 Oct. 2012. http://www.investopedia.com/university/economics/economics3.asp .

"Economy." *Dictionary.com*. Dictionary.com, n.d. Web. 07 Oct. 2012. http://dictionary.reference.com/browse/economy?s=t .

"Francois Fenelon Quotes." *BrainyQuote*. Xplore, n.d. Web. 07 Oct. 2012. http://www.brainyquote.com/quotes/authors/f/francois_fenelon.html .

"Free Trade Agreements." *Free Trade Agreements*. N.p., n.d. Web. 07 Oct. 2012. http://trade.gov/fta/ .

"Free Trade and Globalization." - *Global Issues*. N.p., n.d. Web. 07 Oct. 2012. http://www.globalissues.org/issue/38/free-trade-and-globalization .

"Free Trade." *Dictionary.com*. Dictionary.com, n.d. Web. 07 Oct. 2012. http://dictionary.reference.com/browse/free trade.

"ICasualties | Operation Enduring Freedom | Afghanistan." *ICasualties | Operation Enduring Freedom | Afghanistan*. N.p., n.d. Web. 07 Oct. 2012. http://icasualties.org/oef/ .

"Keynesian Economics." *What Is ? Definition and Meaning*. N.p., n.d. Web. 07 Oct. 2012. http://www.businessdictionary.com/definition/Keynesian-economics.html .

"Lester B. Pearson Quotes." *BrainyQuote*. Xplore, n.d. Web. 07 Oct. 2012. http://www.brainyquote.com/quotes/authors/l/lester_b_pearson.html .

"Microeconomics Versus Macroeconomics." *About.com Economics*. N.p., n.d. Web. 07 Oct. 2012. http://economics.about.com/od/economics-basics/a/Microeconomics-Versus-Macroeconomics.htm .

"Mommy Tongue Political Cartoons." *Political Cartoons*. N.p., n.d. Web. 07 Oct. 2012. http://mommytongue.com/tag/political-cartoons/.

"Our Government." *The White House*. N.p., n.d. Web. 07 Oct. 2012. http://www.whitehouse.gov/our-government .

"Radicalism." *Dictionary.com*. Dictionary.com, n.d. Web. 07 Oct. 2012. http://dictionary.reference.com/browse/radicalism?s=t .

"Republican Party Platform vs Democratic Party Platform." *The Precinct Project's Blog*. N.p., n.d. Web. 07 Oct. 2012. http://theprecinctproject.wordpress.com/republican-party-platform-vs-democrat-party-platform-liberty-vs-secular-socialism/ .

"Supply-side Economics - What Is It and Does ItÂ Work?" *About.com US Economy*. N.p., n.d. Web. 07 Oct. 2012. http://useconomy.about.com/od/fiscalpolicy/p/supply_side.htm .

"Terrorist Attacks in the U.S. or Against Americans." *Infoplease*. Infoplease, n.d. Web. 07 Oct. 2012. http://www.infoplease.com/ipa/A0001454.html .

"Thomas Jefferson Quotes." *BrainyQuote*. Xplore, n.d. Web. 07 Oct. 2012. http://www.brainyquote.com/quotes/authors/t/thomas_jefferson.html.

"Thomas Paine Home." *Thomas Paine Home*. N.p., n.d. Web. 07 Oct. 2012. http://tpnha.keybrick.net/ .

"Thomas Paine Quotes." *BrainyQuote*. Xplore, n.d. Web. 07 Oct. 2012. http://www.brainyquote.com/quotes/authors/t/thomas_paine.html .

"Thomas Paine." *Thomas Paine*. N.p., n.d. Web. 07 Oct. 2012. http://www.ushistory.org/paine/ .

"Treasury: U.S. to Lose $25 Billion on Auto Bailout." *The Detroit News*. N.p., n.d. Web. 07 Oct. 2012. http://www.detroitnews.com/article/20120813/AUTO01/208130392 .

"War On Terror News." *War On Terror News*. N.p., n.d. Web. 07 Oct. 2012. http://waronterrornews.typepad.com/ .

www.ingramcontent.com/pod-product-compliance
Lightning Source LLC
Chambersburg PA
CBHW082151290526

45794CB00008B/3248